HAT TRICK

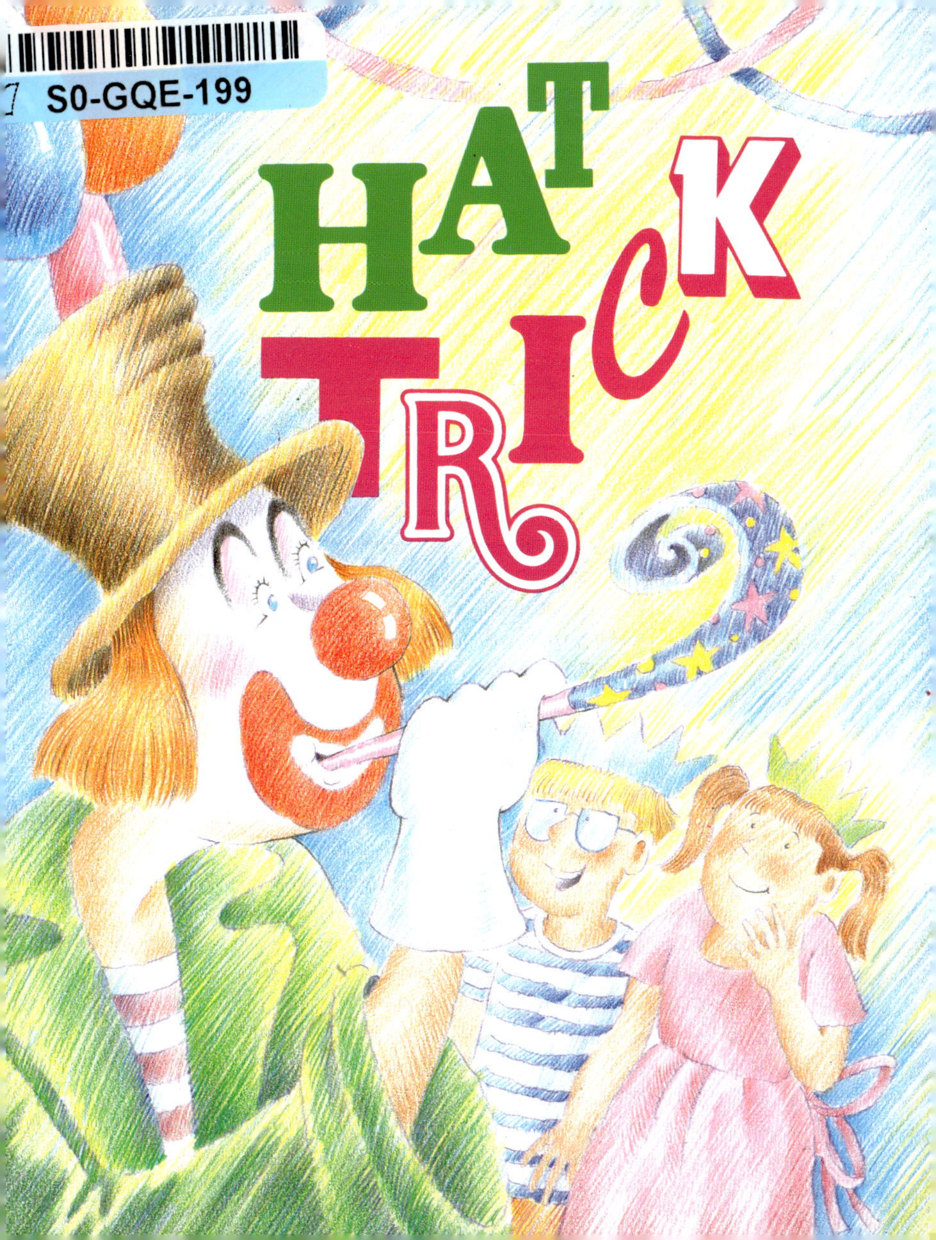

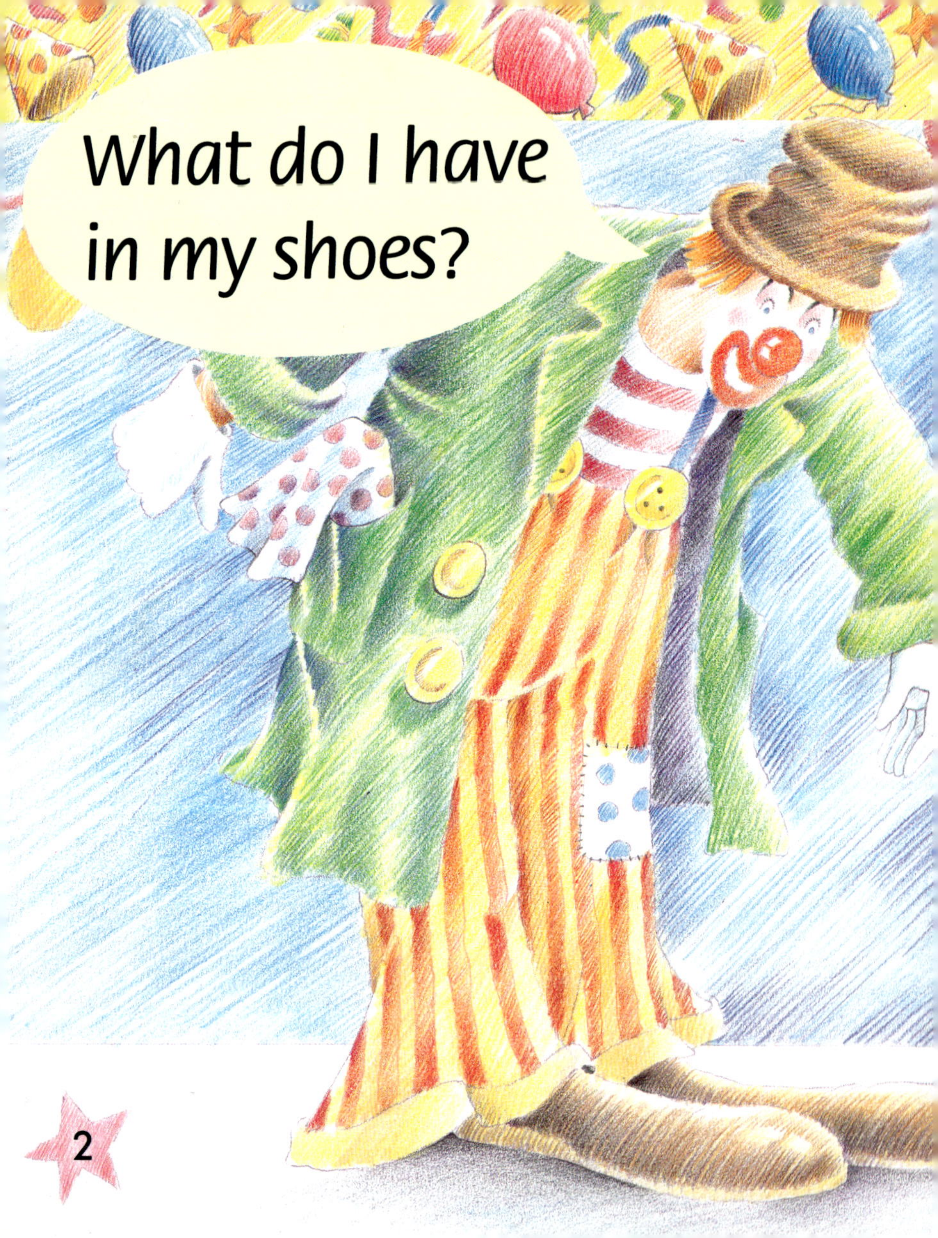
What do I have in my shoes?

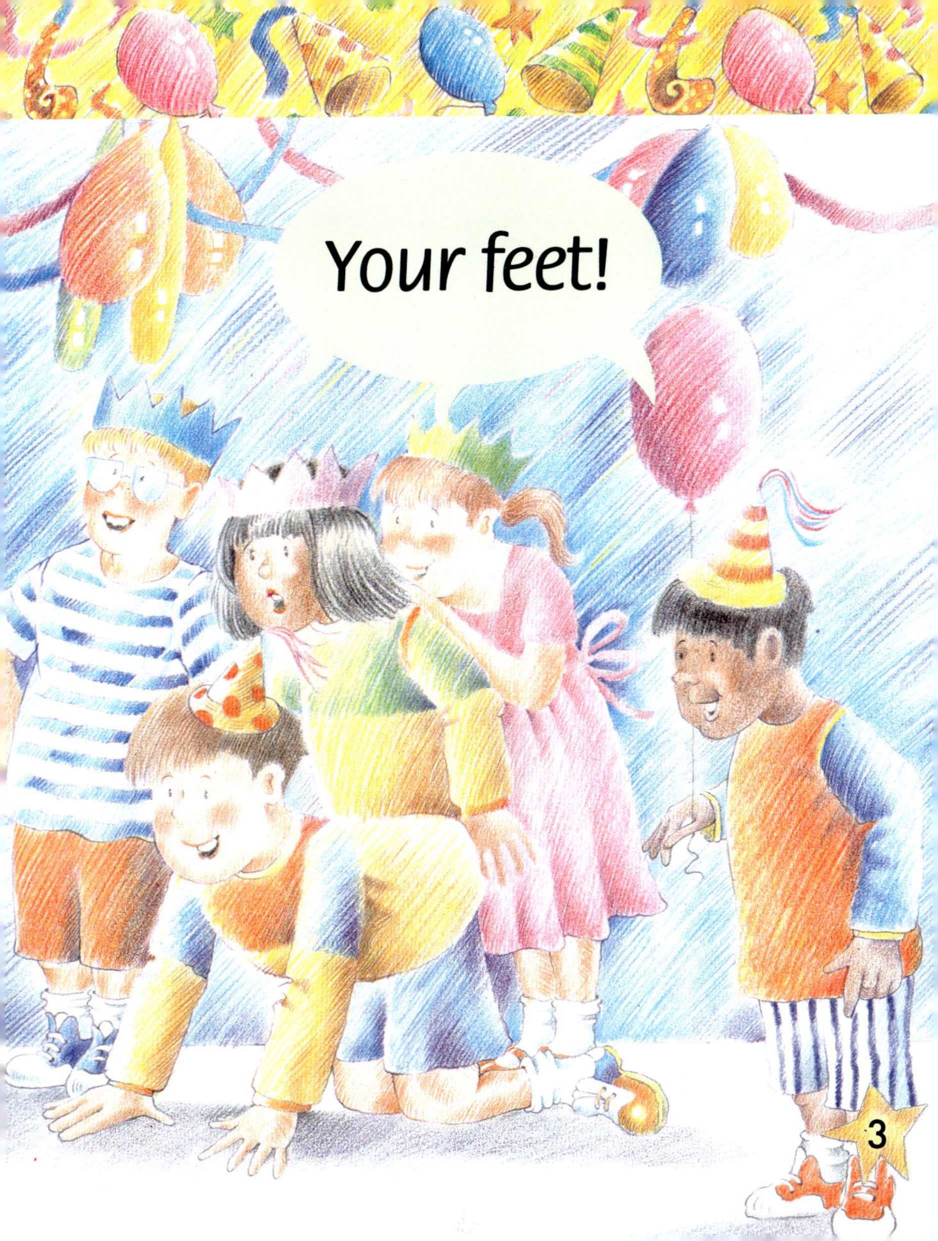
Your feet!

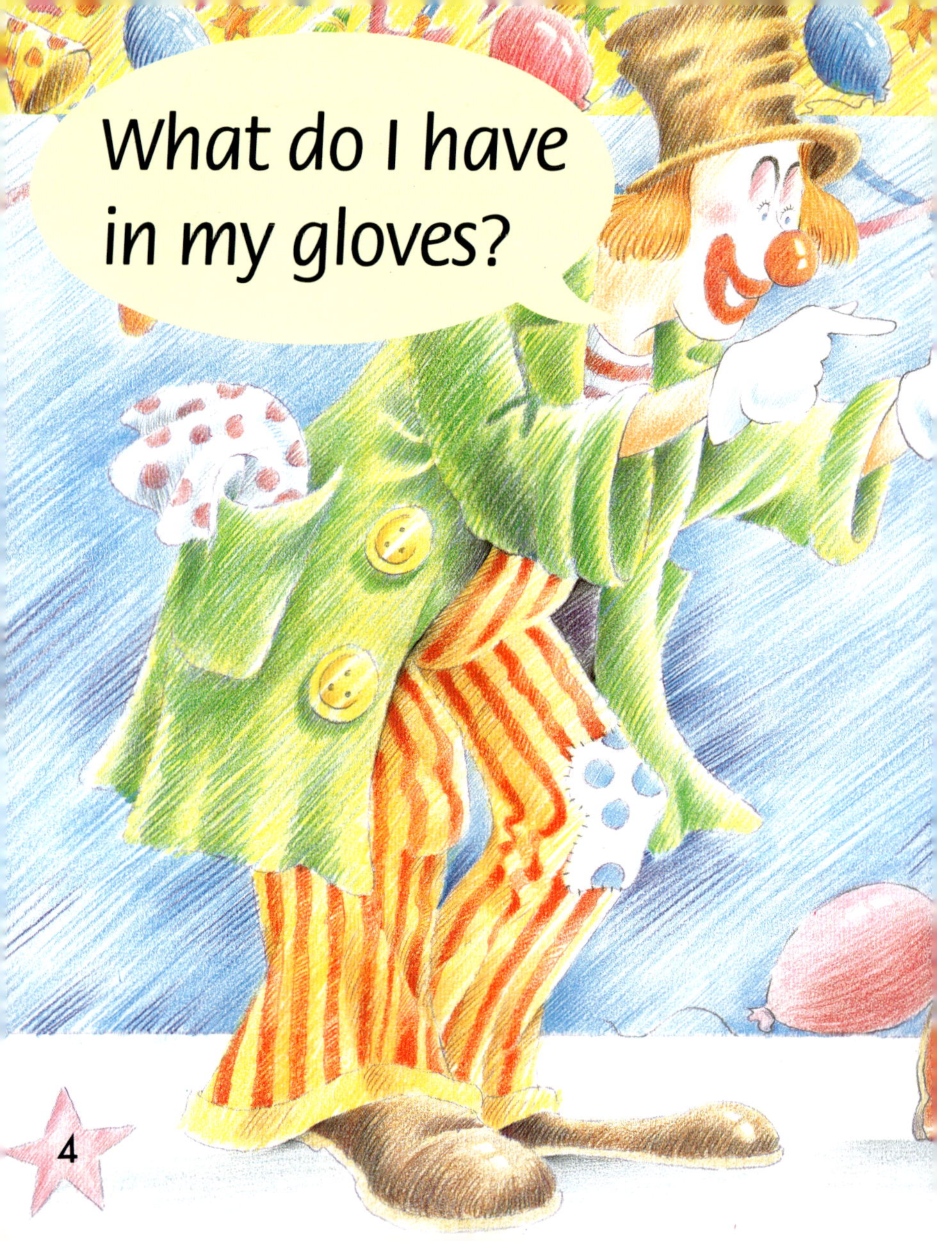
What do I have in my gloves?

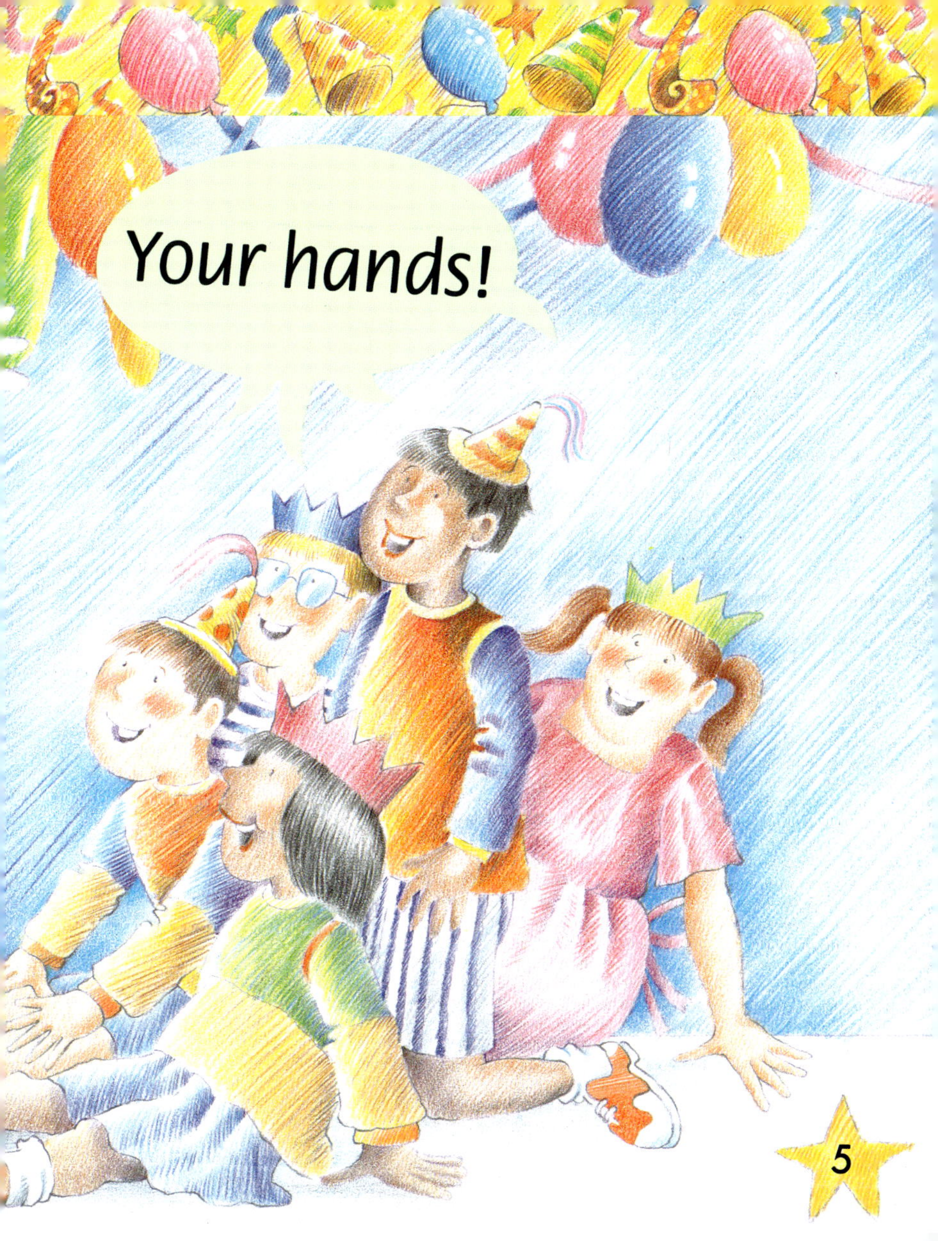
Your hands!

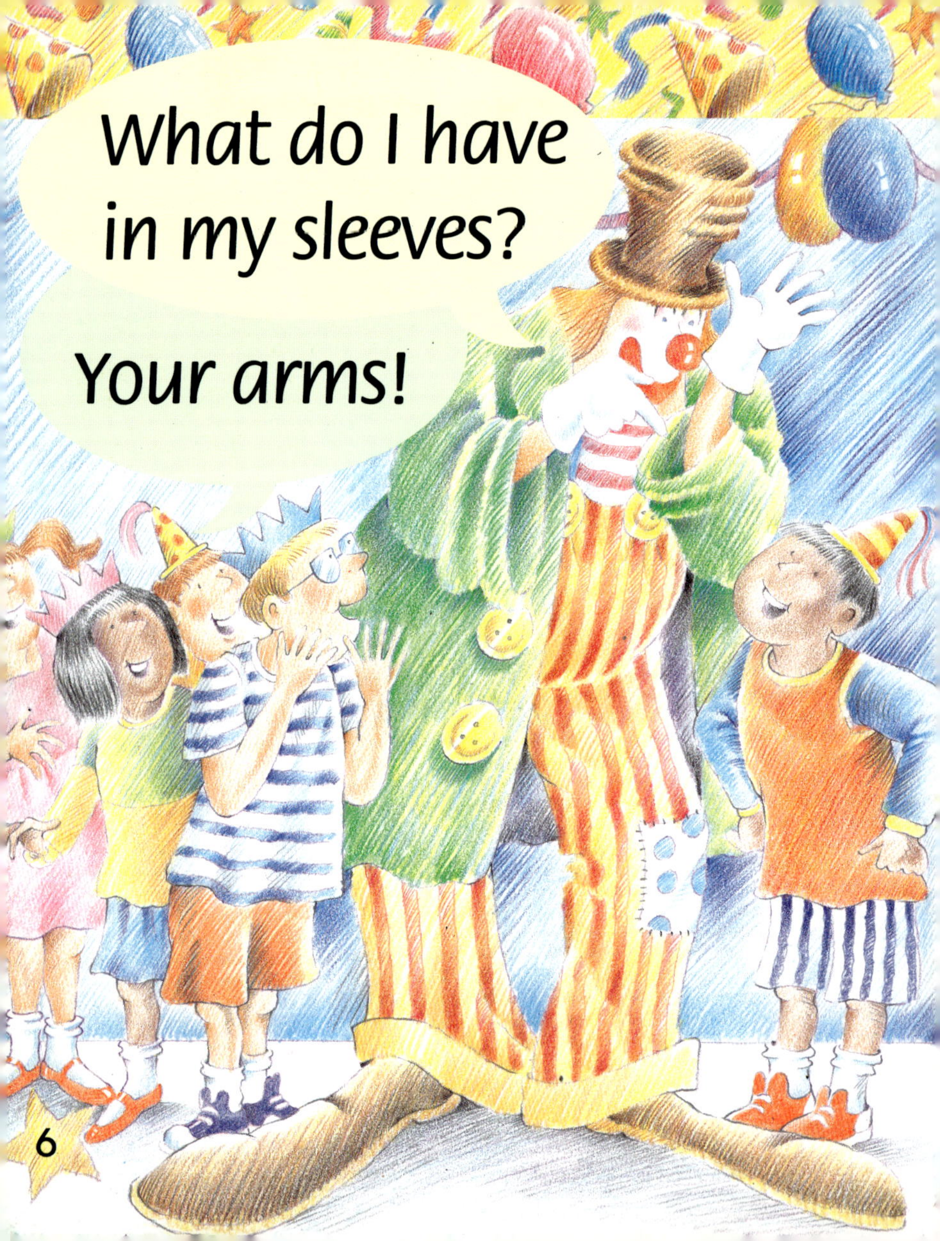
What do I have in my sleeves?
Your arms!

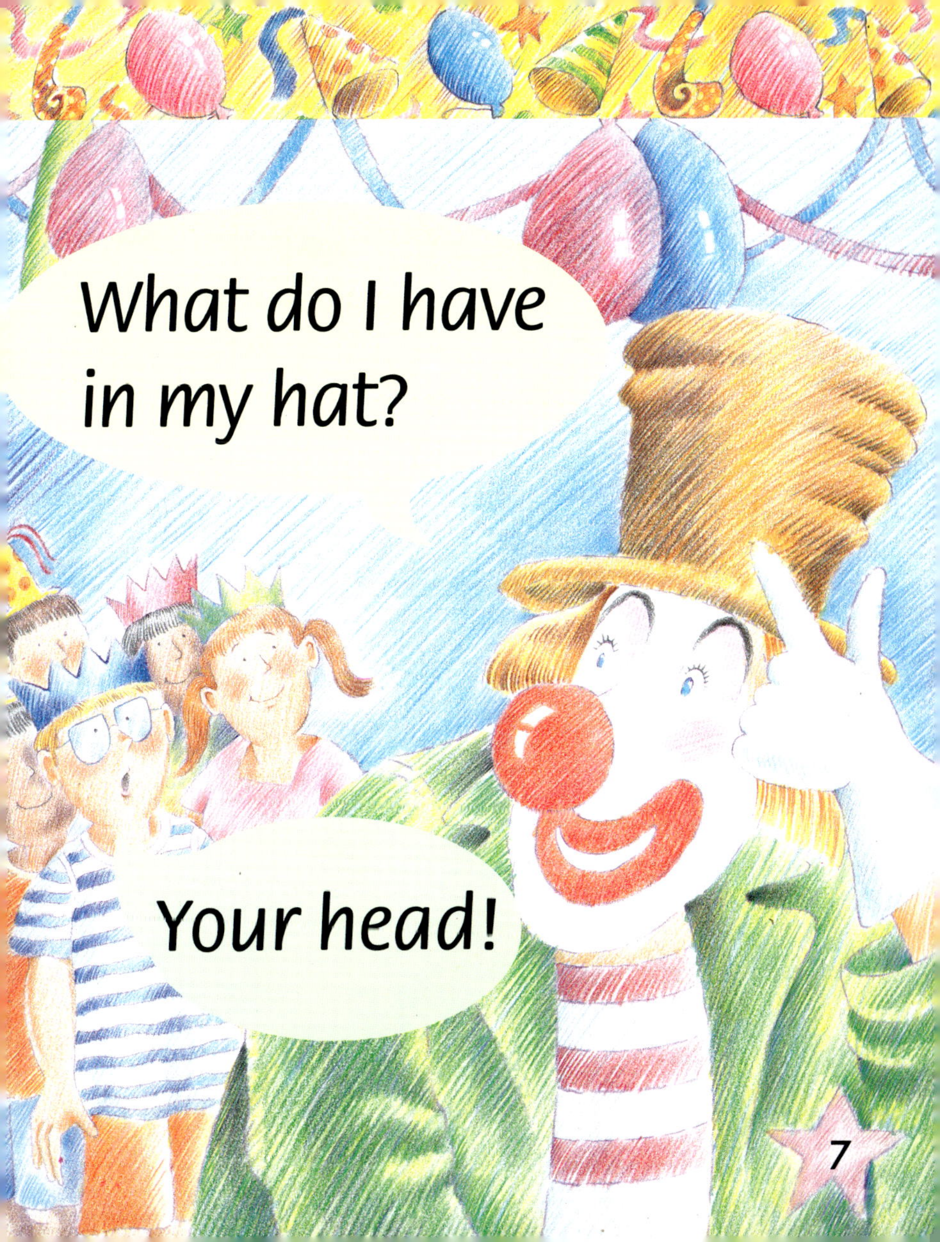
What do I have in my hat?
Your head!

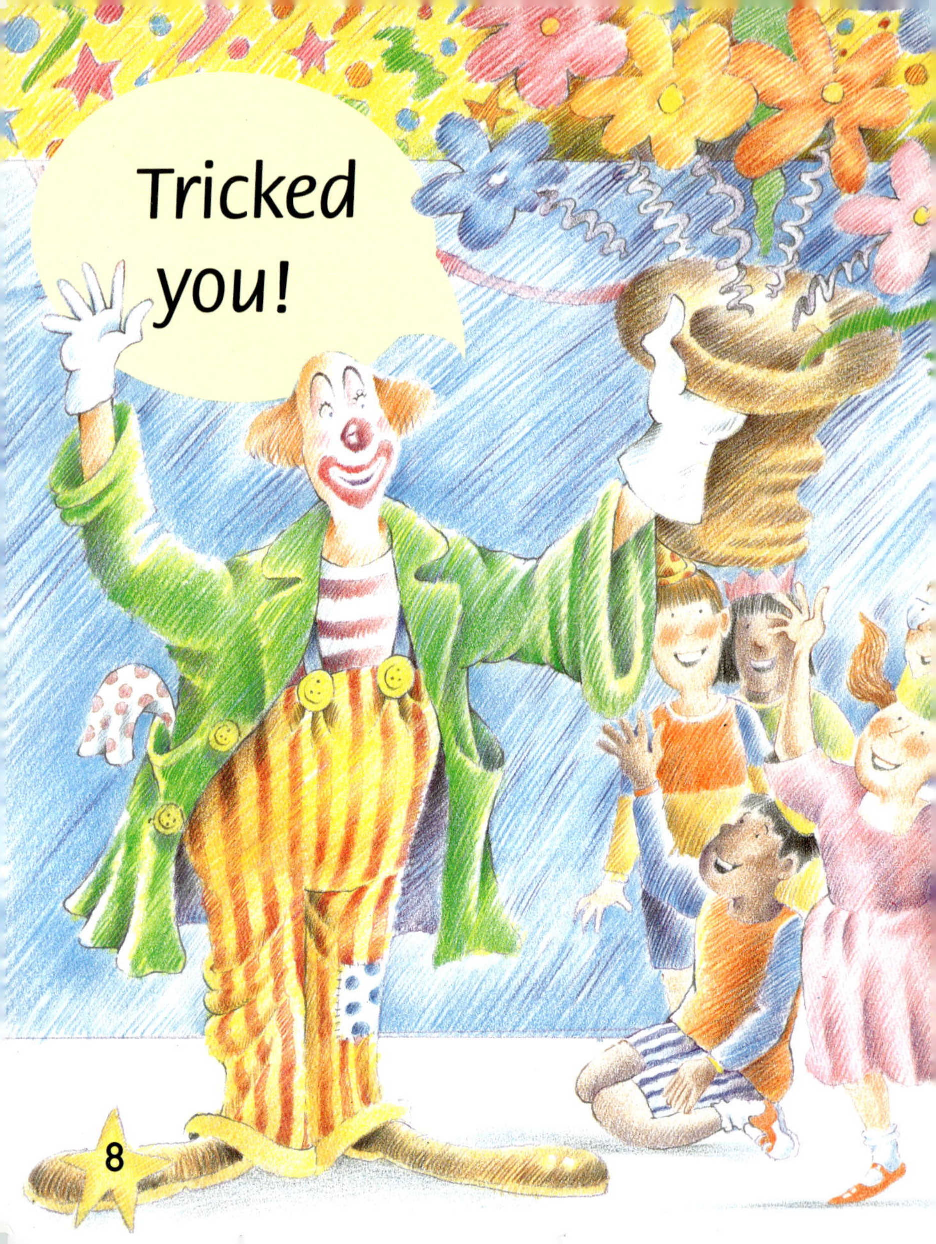
Tricked you!